P9-DFJ-848

LEADING
SUCCESSFUL
CHANGE

8 Keys to Making Change Work

LEADING
SUCCESSFUL
CHANGE

GREGORY P. SHEA, PhD
CASSIE A. SOLOMON

DIGITAL PRESS
Philadelphia

To my wife, Iris, and to our daughters,
Emelyn and Meredith, and to the remarkable
grace that the love of all three has provided me
—GPS

To my colleagues at Christiana Care for their courage
to make real change and to Claire, Katie, and Ben
for teaching me everything I know about real love
—CAS

"You never change things fighting the existing reality. To change something, build a new model that makes the existing model obsolete."
—Richard Buckminster Fuller

"You can't talk your way out of problems you behave yourself into!"
—Stephen R. Covey, *The 7 Habits of Highly Effective People*

"Our ability to adapt is amazing. Our ability to change isn't quite as spectacular."
—Lisa Lutz, *The Spellmans Strike Again*

© 2013 by Shea and Associates, Inc.

Published by Wharton Digital Press
The Wharton School
University of Pennsylvania
3620 Locust Walk
2000 Steinberg Hall-Dietrich Hall
Philadelphia, PA 19104
Email: whartondigitalpress@wharton.upenn.edu
Website: wdp.wharton.upenn.edu

All rights reserved. No part of this book may be reproduced, in any form
or by any means, without written permission of the publisher. Company
and product names mentioned herein are the trademarks or registered
trademarks of their respective owners.

Ebook ISBN: 978-1-61363-024-2
Paperback ISBN: 978-1-61363-019-8

Contents

Introduction
Why Change Initiatives Fail

We live in a world of permanent change—one in which, whatever job title you hold, your real job is in fact change.[1] Yet the majority of efforts to change organizations fail, at enormous cost to these enterprises, their members, customers, and stakeholders. Unfortunately, study after study, decade after decade, reports similar findings, namely that between 50% and 75% of change initiatives fail.[2] The notes for this chapter reference nine such studies, from 1994 to 2010.

Our own travels have also shown us that most change initiatives fail, but whatever the exact number, failure—not success—is the norm. We have known each other for nearly 40 years. We have collaborated in the changing of organizations for more than 20. We help leaders change their organizations in order to reach new performance heights or to adapt to a turbulent environment. In combination, we have done this work for more than 60 years in a wide range of industries: manufacturing, telecom, health care, financial services, power, information services, government, professional service firms, and education. We have worked with US and international companies, start-ups and turnarounds, unionized and non-unionized, and with privately held, publicly traded, and public sector organizations. We have worked at all organizational levels: shop floor, supervisory, managerial, C-suite, and board of directors. For more than 20 years, Greg has served on the faculty and as director of Wharton's semiannual executive education course, Leading Organizational Change. We've written this book because so many people invest so much in changing their work groups, departments, service lines, strategic business units, and organizations, and so many fail, at great cost to organizations, communities, individuals, and families.

Why do so many attempts at organizational change fall short? Certainly not for lack of advice. In fact, there is an entire industry based on exploring this subject, one that touts an array of approaches: tell stories, make change a priority, "walk the talk," and ponder parables about mice and cheese or penguins and icebergs. Many of the most popular books on change address its psychological aspects, and focus on people and their internal states or motivations—and they address both well. These ideas matter and can prove most useful. This psychological perspective taken alone, however, can promote the belief that the success or failure of any given organizational change effort comes down to motivating individual members of the organization and that, correspondingly, a leader's primary job comes down to inspiring the troops. Such a belief can easily lead to unfortunate attributions whenever individuals don't change, namely marking individuals as the problem. The person receives the label "resistant," and perhaps the leader becomes stigmatized as "uninspiring." We contend that altering the attribution and recasting the challenge of resistance significantly improve the likelihood of success.

Nor is failed change necessarily a problem of lack of commitment. You may have led a failed change, whether big or small, even after doing so much right: You did your discovery work. You scanned your world. You developed a sense of urgency. You physically felt the need to change. You made the case (over and over), delineated a strategy, and lined up the powers that be. Yet the change did not happen. It remained uncoupled from the day-to-day operation of the organization, both in design and in execution. The change turned into a shadow of itself or even less and then slipped away, leaving remnants, lost credibility, and numerous casualties. So, just what was the problem? What should you have done differently? What do you *need* to do differently next time?

We contend that change efforts fail for two reasons:

1. Leaders present vague and abstract change objectives: "Improve communication between caregivers and patients and their families" or "Increase profitability." Phrases like these mean different things to different people. They do not specify what to do or how to change. They do not focus on the key aspect of organizational change: the required behavior of individuals.
2. Leaders underestimate the power of the work environment to precipitate or stall change. Many change efforts lack a coordinated or aligned approach to designing the work environment. One aspect of the environment tells people

to make a change, while other aspects of the environment signal to people to continue to act as they always have.

Based on these insights, we present an approach to change that involves focusing on the behaviors that you want from people and designing the work environment to facilitate those behaviors. In this book, we first show you how to think about desired behavior, and then walk you through how to design the work environment using 8 Levers of Change, a comprehensive approach to creating a clear and direct objective and systematically altering the work environment to bring about the desired change.

The ideas presented here derive from the Work Systems Model developed by Shea and Associates, Inc., which is based on systems thinking and sociotechnical theory.[3] Systems thinking is the process of understanding how one part influences both another part and the whole. Nature provides the example of an ecosystem in which each of the various elements—air, water, plants, animals, movement—affects the existence of the other. Like ecosystems, work environments consist of various elements that combine to make a system healthy or unhealthy.

Organizational researchers Eric Trist, Ken Bamforth, and Fred Emery coined the term *sociotechnical systems* in the 1950s, when they worked as consultants at the Tavistock Institute in London.[4] (Later, Trist and Emery continued their work at the University of Pennsylvania.) *Sociotechnical* refers to the interrelatedness of social and technical aspects of an organization. The Work Systems Model focuses on the behaviors that change should produce and the changes in the various aspects of the environment or work systems necessary to facilitate those behaviors. Once change leaders learn to be system thinkers, they can begin to see that some systems facilitate the desired change and some inhibit it.

In the chapters that follow, we will show how to identify *not* the behaviors you are seeking to change, but rather, those behaviors you want to *see* in place when your change is complete. We'll introduce you to the 8 Levers of Change, and offer compelling case studies in which those Change Levers have been pulled in creative combinations to defy the odds, break the failure norm, and bring real and much-needed change to enterprises in danger of being swept away by the swirling turmoil every business faces today.

Please don't misunderstand: transforming an organization isn't for the faint of heart. Doing so takes patience, discipline, even courage. But it can be done. It has been done successfully, time and again, following the approach we lay out here. And you can do it.

Finally, some advice on how to read this book. Pick a change initiative you've championed, led, or were caught up in that didn't work out. Make some notes to yourself on why you think it failed and keep those at hand. Next, in another set of notes, create a profile for a significant change you would now like to make. Maybe globalization has created yet another threat or opportunity. Perhaps shifts in taxes, tariffs, regulations, or a political regime have cracked open, redefined, or closed off markets. You might need to act because a major competitor has demonstrated an unanticipated strength or weakness—or because your own organization has developed or lost a key capacity.

Regardless, jot down a few comments about the nature of the change you seek and why it matters to you today. Then, as you move through this book, consult and expand your two sets of notes. Test the contents of this book against your own experience. See if a future begins to unfold that is better than the past failure. We think one will.

The times are not just a-changin'. Our era is dominated by the reality that change is constant. We all need to get better at it—and sooner rather than later. You owe yourself and the people depending upon your leadership no less. We offer you this book in that spirit.

Gregory P. Shea, PhD
sheag@wharton.upenn.edu

Cassie A. Solomon
cassie@thenewgroupconsulting.com

CHAPTER 1

So, You Say You Want a Revolution? *Focus on Behavior and Change the Work Environment*

Halloran, a US-based specialty chemical manufacturer, had a Big Problem. The company had manufacturing facilities all over the world—Asia, Latin America, North America, and Europe—and sourced its raw materials from thousands of small global suppliers. Management had created a global supply chain so complicated that it all but precluded lowering raw material costs. To remain competitive, Halloran needed to change.[1]

Tom Keating served as the Halloran executive in charge of purchasing, and he had a Big Solution to the Big Problem. Halloran would henceforth outsource logistics completely to independent contractor Straight Arrow, and Straight Arrow would create warehouses in various regions to serve Halloran's scattered manufacturing zones, transport raw materials to be held in those warehouses, centralize their purchase as much as possible to China, and carry the cost of holding the inventory close to the local manufacturing need. The consultants would manage the planning forecasts and maintain a three-month pipeline of materials. Halloran would gain a great supply chain, and Straight Arrow would get a new business model.

"No question about it," Keating confidently told his bosses and direct reports, "this arrangement will eliminate the long lead times for material coming from Asia, increase supply chain predictability, and decrease cost by leveraging world-class supply chain expertise." In fact, many of the ingredients for a successful change initiative looked to be in place, and there was no question about the urgency, given global competition. Keating and the senior consultant from Straight Arrow went on a global "road show" to explain the concept to operations leaders in every region. They believed that if they showed leadership commitment to the program, brought a quality plan to the field, and communicated it effectively, then one and all would see its merits and a smooth implementation would follow. Eighteen months after launch, in the spring of 2008, Keating's supply chain leadership team held a retreat to evaluate the initiative's success. People agreed: it was not a pretty sight. Halloran operations people thought the Straight Arrow consultants arrogant, often mistaken, and far too expensive. Allocation of the cost of the program went to the plant manager's P&L, but allocation of raw materials savings went to the corporate scorecard. In other words, program cost and program reward went to different stakeholders. In addition, local purchasing agents didn't want to give up their decision-making authority or relationships with local suppliers they had nurtured for years.

The Straight Arrow execs couldn't understand Halloran's foot-dragging. And Keating couldn't jawbone or intimidate either side into cooperating. Six months later he was gone. His replacement struggled mightily to overhaul the initiative, but to no avail. A year on, with the global economy in a sharp downturn, Halloran's executive committee canceled the Straight Arrow contract and the global sourcing program. In the end, after 36 months of struggle, Halloran's competitors had leapfrogged it, and Halloran had little positive to show for the considerable money, time, and effort expended.

"There was nothing wrong with this idea," one of the principals on the operation side told us when we sat down to do a postmortem with him. "The execution was a disaster." Why? Simply stated, the change leaders did not articulate what they wanted, so they could not design to achieve it. The change process was, in the end, not about software or inventory protocols. It was about behavior, but it did not include identifying the desired behavioral changes within operations or at the plant level. This lack of a clear behavioral end state inevitably meant a lack of focus. A fine conceptualization of a supply chain at corporate came to less than naught because people on the ground didn't use it. Why? Because local realities argued against it.

We're Only Human

The human being is a midsize omnivorous mammal that has invested large amounts of evolutionary energy developing a particularly large and complex brain. This brain enables us to scan our world in both simple and sophisticated ways and to fashion responses to it. We can work in the concrete and in the abstract, and we can construct complex social systems that allow us to gain the power born of large, coordinated groupings or organizations. We study and experiment and learn precisely so we can alter our behavior and adjust to new circumstances. In fact, much of our conscious mind apparently exists to perceive and to manage social reality.

All these qualities enable us to adapt proactively to our environment. No, we are not the equal of cockroaches or retroviruses in this regard, but any creature that can prosper in tropical, temperate, and frigid climates, in arid environs, and in land dominated by water surely deserves the description "adaptable."

To understand just how "adaptable" we are, take a look around you. The average workplace is filled with people sitting in cubicles or bent over laptops, trying to figure out what to do next. Precious few of us set out to demonstrate our incompetence, to fail. Motivational and behavioral theorists might differ on various counts, but virtually everyone agrees that human beings try to impact their environment and make it work for them. Even the smallest of children demonstrate this tendency to reach out (literally) and shape their world. Adapting and overcoming are central parts of who and what we are.

Why, then, is organizational change so difficult? Why do leaders fret so much about it and management gurus roll out new theories, seemingly on the hour, about how to accomplish it? The answer is fairly simple: far too often, we forget that we are, in fact, big-brained mammals attending to our environment, especially our social environment, in order to make it work for us. Like Halloran's Tom Keating, we design change to accomplish great goals, to make sweeping organizational reforms, to seize expansive new markets, and to survive in old, shrinking ones. But in doing so, we ignore the reality that until we have changed individual behavior, we have changed little or nothing at all.

Change Is All About the Lead Dog, Right?

So contends a host of renowned experts. If a leader walks the talk and manages by walking around, if he or she communicates by crafting poignant elevator speeches and relentlessly delivering the message of change, then successful change itself is sure to come. After all, just look at the lead dog—or ape, or penguin, depending on the theory of the day: yelp, bark, and whine enough, and the others are sure to follow.

That is all well and good for animal packs, and it helps with humans, too. But by itself, the lead-animal theory is woefully insufficient for changing large organizations or large parts of organizations. Leaders modeling behavior and talking the case for change can indeed help enterprises transform. But the corporate alpha dog doesn't sit among the pack. He appears only briefly, via dispatch or WebEx or the rare visit—something like Tom Keating's "road show." Soon, the appearance fades and the banners droop. The workers, the managers, and even the executives look around to see if their environment has changed, if the tried-and-true behaviors that made their world work will continue to do so. If they won't, fine; it's time to adapt. If they will, really, why bother to change?

How, then, does one change an organization—be it a company, business unit, service line, department, or work unit? *By changing the work environment around the people whose behavior you seek to change.* Therein lies the key to successful, embedded, and sustained change: alter the environment, and people will adapt to it. Call it a species strength. We behave based on the reality we perceive. Therefore, design a work environment that requires different behaviors. Then concentrate on helping people do what they do so well: namely, adapt. Design work environments that inspire desired behaviors, and you have already won a large part of the change battle. This amounts to "pulling" versus "pushing" organizational change.

Think Environment

Behavior at work is "overdetermined." This amounts to a fancy way of saying that people generally do what they do for a variety of reasons. Changing what people do, then, must address multiple influences. Anyone who has tried to begin or sustain an exercise regimen knows that those simple, straightforward, and unarguably beneficial behavioral changes require other changes. The challenge here isn't in achieving clarity about the desired behavior—e.g., exercising for at least 30 minutes four times per week. Nor is it in understanding the benefits, such as lower blood pressure and a healthier and probably longer life. The challenge is constructing a world around the individual trying to change: changes in relationships, work, eating patterns, schedules, lifestyle, feedback or information, measurement, rewards, skills, and support systems. For example, join a gym close to your home to increase the likelihood that you will use it. Ante up, make the investment, and buy the right clothing and gear, including a bag to carry it in. Set an alarm that reminds you when to go to the gym. Log and measure your progress on a regular basis, posting it in full view. Invent small rewards as you reach various milestones in the process (number of trips to the gym) and outcome (duration of your exercise or decrease in blood pressure). Create social rewards, too: post your progress online for your friends to see, organize a group of people who are committed to the same goals, or send texts to your primary care physician. According to John Tierney, coauthor of *Willpower: Rediscovering the Greatest Human Strength,* one-third of people who make New Year's resolutions will have dropped them by the end of January, and by July more than half of those original resolutions will have lapsed.[2] Depend on your willpower alone, and you will probably slenderize only your odds of success.

Simply put, a desired behavior or set or pattern of behaviors must *make sense to people,* not abstractly and not for a moment of inspiration, but each day, every day. To make sense at work, the desired behaviors need to fit the work environment. They need to help people get what they want from the world around them. They need to work.

If you know what you want people to do, then how might you design their world to help them to do it? The question seems straightforward, even obvious, and examples abound of successful efforts to do just that, and not only in the business world. Let's return to the world of fitness. Fitbit has developed a successful business by offering an approach to weight loss and fitness consistent with the approach just described. Fitbit is a lightweight device that monitors your physical activity, calorie intake, weight, and sleep. It continuously measures and updates. It also provides easy access to measurement information and the ability to download the data. Users earn rewards (merit badges) as they use the information to make healthier decisions. A user can readily acquire the necessary skills to use the device. The manufacturer provides online support, and communities of users have sprung up, providing both competition and support. In other words, a modest technological innovation provides the occasion for altering the user's behavior through a coordinated altering of his environment.

But (witness Halloran) altering the ground-level environment is rarely the first thing that comes to the mind of organizational change implementers. As in the case of Tom Keating, they envision strategic shifts that will be game changers, or at least company savers. Next, they fill in the mechanics that will get them where they want to be (holding warehouses, strategic partners, and so on). And finally, maybe, they give some thought to the on-the-ground agents of change (i.e., the workers) who actually hold success or failure in their very hands. It's only when the promised benefits *don't* materialize that those involved come to see that the entire change process began at the wrong end.

As one Halloran executive told us, "The model was quite vast: plants and people in different parts of the world, all people who needed to understand what we were doing. Every time we tried to roll it out in a new plant, months would go by before we came to any result; it became a self-fulfilling prophecy. The whole program relies on implementation. If you get it implemented, the dollars will flow. If you don't get it implemented, it will just cost you money."

Much of this book considers how to create an aligned environment that will drive implementation and embed the desired organizational change, but changing the work environment alone will seldom yield the desired change. Rather, one must change the work environment purposefully in *light* of carefully considered and specified desired behavioral change. "We'll know it when we see it," the mantra of some change implementers, most likely will not get the job done. Elaborate the future world. Use that elaboration to guide construction of a work environment that will generate a pull or trajectory in the direction of that world.

Focus on Behavior

How do you optimize the possibility of successfully implementing change? By defining exactly what you wish to create and by doing so using as much behavioral specificity as possible—and as little jargon as possible, too. Phrases such as "increased interunit communication" or "enhanced field and staff collaboration" have a comforting blandness to them, but they almost always serve to blur, not sharpen, the picture.

The market may have presented an opportunity or posed a threat. Your organization's evolution may have enabled or hamstrung a noteworthy move. No matter the cause or the reason, organizational change entails changing human behavior. It entails making certain key behaviors a reliable and regular part of organizational operation—that is, of "how the place works." The question for the change leader comes down to this: What behaviors must occur, how must people act, in order to make the change succeed? What's the story you want told about the way you and your people will operate in the future? What's different? And what in the work environment still stands in the way?

Changing organizations comes down to changing human behavior. Design of the work environment or system design, in turn, drives human behavior in complex entities such as organizations. One might well argue that human organizations are systems of systems. To change them requires less magical imagery and Herculean effort and more careful consideration of just what a leader seeks to create with change and how to align the corporate or business unit or department work environment to produce that desired, even longed-for change. To increase the odds of successful change, increase the discipline of thought, planning, and execution, beginning with clarity of what behavior the leader wants and the system changes necessary to produce it.

Connecting Intent and Implementation

Therefore, to create successful change, always remember these two tenets:

1. Focus on the behaviors you want from people.
2. Design the work environment to foster those behaviors.

Focusing on behaviors and the work environments that support them does not mean that ideals, values, principles, motivations, and other more high-minded issues do not count. Of course they do, but a leader who focuses on behaviors is recognizing and taking advantage of the fact that behavior constitutes the most important currency of exchange within human systems: You do something or you do not do something. I forward sales leads or I do not. I look for customer input or I do not. I actively collaborate with my peers on product redesign or I do not. My behavior and that of other organizational members determines whether a given change initiative lives or dies. Behavior is the connective tissue between strategy and action, between intent and implementation. Behavior comprises culture.

Hence, successful change comes down to identifying the key behaviors that, if they occur reliably and regularly, indicate that a desired change has taken hold. A detailed, even granular, vision of the future can dramatically increase the odds of getting there. Abstract or ephemeral visions wrapped in corporate speak do not. A specific vision can provide local meaning. It can clarify communication, motivate and direct action, aid planning, facilitate debriefing, guide revising, and revitalize by occasioning celebration of progress. Above all, a specific behavioral vision helps change leaders redesign the work environment to foster the behaviors and the change. In the next chapter, we introduce a framework for constructing scenes that help you identify the behaviors you want to see.

CHAPTER 2

Make a Scene
Envision What You Want

G öran Carstedt, president of IKEA North America, sum-
moned his top executives to a large meeting room to share
his strategic plan. They arrived prepared for a flashy PowerPoint
presentation complete with charts and graphs. Instead, Carstedt
told them a story about a mother. He depicted a detailed scene
of her and her husband getting two kids off to school in the
morning. She gets up, makes coffee, wakes up the children,
makes breakfast, and so on. Then he paused and moved to the
heart of the matter: "Our strategic plan is to make that family's
life easier by providing them with convenient and affordable
household items in an accessible location. Period."[1]

Carstedt, in short, wanted IKEA to enter the scene, to
populate it with IKEA-supplied usefulness that customers would
appreciate having in their homes as they conducted their daily
lives. He wanted his executives, in effect, to write IKEA into
their customers' story in a way that improved the story for the
characters that populated it. Brilliant! As Carmen Nobel, senior
editor at Harvard Business School Working Knowledge, notes,
"IKEA has made very clear choices about who they will be and
to whom they will matter, and why."[2]

Clarity of purpose in any endeavor—from invading Afghanistan to marketing an MP3 player to orienting a global home furnishing empire—avoids wasting resources such as time, money, effort, and communication. No surprise there. The same holds true for organizational change. If the desired change were to take hold, what would you see as you walked through a work area? What would you hear as the proverbial fly on the wall? Hover for a moment over the flow of information or product or service. How is the decision making on given matters unfolding? How does information move, and from where to where?

A change leader who hasn't thought through these questions hasn't prepared adequately to move to implementation— no matter how grand the change scheme, no matter how beautiful the flow charts or how heartfelt the calls for "enhanced communication," "a culture of safety," or "dedication to innovation." Absent a clear set of end behaviors on the horizon, a crew that starts rowing, perhaps even with vigor, but with little idea where they should head, will likely end up exhausted and disillusioned.

Change leaders need to focus on behavior, desired behaviors in particular. Easy to say. Intuitively obvious, perhaps. Yet doing so takes time and effort. Doing so also facilitates clearer focus and crisper implementation. The odds of success drop if you don't know what success looks like.

Lights, Cameras, Action

There's no "best way" to imagine the future. For some people, meditation helps. Others get there more deliberately—with a legal pad in hand or by sketching a time line on a laptop. However you travel, bear two principles in mind. First, move far enough into the future to uncouple yourself from the major constraints of the moment. For executives, this usually means moving at least five years and perhaps ten years out. For managers, two to four years might prove sufficient. Starting at a specific moment and working back to the present produces more creative thinking. Second, assume the world you desire has come to pass. This helps make the unreal more concrete and enables greater, easier specification of that world. With these principles taken as given, the process that follows should help you find the desired future and delineate the end behaviors needed to get there.

Envision a Direction

Start Big

Just because change is difficult doesn't mean it has to be timid. In fact, bold change initiatives can prove easier to pull off than incremental ones, because they force—or should force—change leaders to think systemwide, not just about processes but about the people who implement them. As noted earlier, there was nothing inherently wrong with Halloran's supply chain initiative. The failure was one of scope. Tom Keating envisioned only half of what the future required. He could see his supply chain working like a perfectly made Swiss watch, but he forgot that the parts that would make it hum were people, not gears and springs. Successfully implementing widespread change requires successfully altering widespread patterns of behavior across large numbers of people reacting to a multitude of cues from the work world around them. Begin there.

Focus on Intent

What specifically are you trying to get your business to do? More local problem solving? A broader, deeper commitment to quality or safety? Ongoing refinement of production or delivery processes? Enhanced attention to product innovation? A dedication to customer service and intimacy? Regardless of whether the underlying push or pull comes from outside the organization or from within it, what's the end purpose? If you can't state it in one simple sentence, you're not ready to imagine what it will look like if and when it's achieved.

Identify Critical Roles

Which organization members will most contribute to realizing your intent? And don't stop with the executive suites. The goal here is to think ground level, those proverbial trenches. Titles and job descriptions do not matter; function and behavior do. Salespeople switching their focus from volume to customer satisfaction may provide the most powerful insight into the required work system changes. Or perhaps envisioning housekeepers moving from pure maintenance activity to customer representatives will enable the most acute (and painful) analysis of the current work environment. Or receptionists migrating from check-in portals to point-of-contact client problem solvers. It's the future. Anything can come true.

Focus on Behavior, Create a Scene

Become the Screenwriter of Your Future

Imagine a scene involving key roles. How might that account manager interact with production or marketing in another line of business or in a different part of the globe? What triggers the interaction—new, readily available information? If so, then of what sort? Why does the account manager care? Why does the person on the other end care? How can you tell? Who decides on a course of action, if any? Lay out all of what transpires as if it has occurred and you are merely recording the action. To make the scene come alive, and to force yourself into its details, pay particular attention to:

- *Person.* Think about a particular person in a particular role in your organization, e.g., a purchasing agent in a local manufacturing plant at Halloran, a nurse manager in charge of a patient care unit, or an engineer in the scheduling department at the Chicago Transit Authority. How will the change affect that person's day-to-day job or even just a particular set of activities? What does that person do today? What will she do differently tomorrow?
- *Flow chart.* Create a step-by-step chart that helps you tell the story of the imagined change. What happens first? What happens next? Who takes what actions?
- *Story.* Tell the story from the perspective of the focal person or persons. Relate the story in the first person: "I am a purchasing manager, and when I get to work in the morning, I have an urgent message from my internal customer in sales…" What do you say? What do you do next? Whom do you talk to? What information do you request and receive, and in what form?
- *Props.* Mock up a sample report, dashboard, or meeting agenda for this brave new world. The specificity in and of itself is not the point; it only serves to illustrate. For

example, if you are a nurse manager in charge of an inpatient hospital unit, look at the data you might receive every morning based on a new tool. Having a sample report in hand makes it easier to talk with the "change target" (i.e., the owner and controller of the desired behavior) about just what the desired change is and, at least as important, what needs to happen to drive and embed that change in the unit.

Repeat

Focus on other key roles and do the same. Perhaps one scene involves a proactive middle management group fashioning the best approach to handling account receivables, another delineates an idealized performance review session for vice presidents, and still another describes a consideration of capital allocation or the desired approach to determining space needs.

Stay with It

What constitutes sufficient work on scenes? The Pareto principle can help here—have you depicted the right 20% of the change, enough to make you confident that with that 20% in place, the other 80% will follow?[3] If yes, then move on. If not, then develop the scene further or construct a new scene. Aim for critical mass, for enough key scenes to define the trajectory of the change and its behavioral nature. Constructing scenes often proves the most difficult step in designing change. People want to rush to the work environment and implementation. Yet clarity here speeds the work there. Get as specific as possible. As the Amish say, to go fast, go slow first.

An Example of Scene Construction... In Situ

In 2011 we worked with a large regional teaching hospital with one of the busiest emergency rooms (ERs) on the East Coast of the United States.[4] Volume just kept climbing. The decline in reimbursement for primary care in the United States and the rising number of uninsured meant that here, as elsewhere, more people made more frequent use of the ER. It is, essentially, the front door of the hospital.

The ER staff faced a common and painful challenge: it took far too long to evaluate and transfer critically ill patients to the intensive care unit (ICU). Only about four or five such patients appeared on any day—a small percentage of the ER's total load—but they consumed a disproportionate share of the department's resources. Intensive care means intensive nursing care, ideally a two-to-one patient-to-nurse ratio, much different and much more resource intensive than the normal five-to-one staffing in ERs. Treating these patients pulled nurses from other important work, which increased wait time in the ER for other patients. Research clearly shows that long wait times in the ER do nothing good for patient outcomes, especially for those who are critically ill.

Eighteen months earlier, the hospital had taken a run at this problem, assembling a multidisciplinary team to study it. Eventually, the team engaged a "lean reengineering" expert to help them reinvent the process so that the sickest patients got onto an "express track" to the ICU upstairs. At first the new process showed encouraging results: the average wait time for patients assigned to the express track dropped dramatically. But further evaluation showed that only 20% of the ICU patients managed to make it into the express category while the rest still waited too long in the ER. The hospital's associate chair of medicine, Dr. Ted Robler, saw with dismay that one critically ill patient had waited 31 hours for a bed to open up in the ICU. *Thirty-one hours?* A traditional approach to change had not yielded the necessary results for enough people.

Robler issued a straightforward challenge to his team: figure out what it would take to get *all* critically ill patients out of the ER in half the current average time. "Impossible," the team responded, due to the complexity of the problem. There were capacity issues (not enough beds in the ICU) and cultural differences between the way ER physicians, hospitalists (physicians who specialize in treating hospitalized patients), and ICU physicians practice and make decisions. Communication barriers and conflicts also divided the two sets of relevant nurses, ER and ICU. And the conditions of the patients change as they wait. Some patients improve, and others deteriorate; hence the issue of "right patient, right bed, right time" can shift over time. Robler liked and understood the idea that "big" change could prove more likely to be successful than incremental change, especially for complex problems. Painfully, after nine months of a reengineering process, he led his department back to the drawing board.

We had worked together before, and he contacted us. Together, we set out to try a more systems-based approach to the challenge. The group learned the Work Systems Model and used it to generate the following scene:

> We see a team of people working together down in the ER, nurses from the ICU and from the Emergency Department

working side by side. They are talking about a critically ill patient and discussing his care. They clearly know one another well and are working well together, helping one another out. There's a physician's assistant (PA) from the ICU in the scene conferring with a doctor from the ER; the ICU PA then confers about orders with the nurse. Then the PA calls upstairs to make sure a bed is available, and gives instructions about moving another patient upstairs who no longer needs intensive care. "We need the bed now," she says quietly. This patient is already "owned" by the ICU, regardless of geography. If he must wait for a bed, the ICU team will stay with him until one is available. The process happens very quickly and calmly. As the patient leaves with the ICU clinicians, the clinicians say to their ER colleagues, "'Thanks, we'll be right back down to help with that patient in Core C." And everyone smiles.

Seemingly simple enough. Yet hospitals do not traditionally work this way. Hospitals are organized by special functions such as intensive care or emergency medicine, and the doctors and nurses in each functional area have their own similar training, passions, skills, and unique ways of caring for patients. Typically, each department works together in one physical location and may even use different computer systems. Owing to their relative isolation, the departments have invented different metrics to measure their success, and they track them in separate budgets and with separate scorecards. Little wonder that when patients are moved from one location to another, valuable information is too often lost with each handoff. Loss of potentially vital information creates the risk of patient harm—a risk that expands dramatically with already critically sick patients.

With that background in hand, look again at how this scenario alters all that. Departments better understand each other's culture. Doctors, PAs, and nurses from the ER and ICU work cooperatively and side by side. Personal and organizational impediments to getting patients from the ER (the hospital's front door) to the ICU, its critical care unit, have vanished. There's even time, in the midst of this possibly life-and-death situation, for a smile. Individually, the behaviors seem small, but in aggregate they constitute a very different world for both staff and patients, a much more desirable world.

Scenes can run from a paragraph, like this one, to several pages. They can capture an instant or relate a meeting or a full encounter. They can stand alone or, again, like this one, fit within a portfolio of scenes. Regardless, a scene forms the basis for the analysis necessary to answer the question: What needs to change to make that scene occur reliably and repeatedly, again and again—i.e., to get the desired change to happen?

Something very like that scene took place a few months later. The hospital leadership wanted to pilot the new design first because the boldness of the change alarmed them and required additional resources. The nurse manager of the ICU confessed to us that, at first, going down to the ER seemed "like going to the dark side of the moon." However, during the pilot, the ICU teams adapted to working in the ER and discovered that doing so wasn't as bad as feared. In fact, the collaboration proved satisfying, and the patients benefited. The program expanded to full operation.

The change pilot halved the ER time for critically ill patients and demonstrated that it was feasible—even enjoyable—to bring an ICU team to work in the ER. Just months into the full implementation of the change, the ER time for critically ill patients has been reduced by 25-35%, a dramatic improvement. Remarkably this result has occurred even on days when the ICU had no beds available! And, as envisioned, relations between clinicians changed from difficult to collaborative, becoming working, problem-solving professional relationships. The change continues to unfold as we go to press. Predictably, Dr. Robler's stock has risen.

In the next chapter, we turn to the task of identifying necessary changes in the work environment.

CHAPTER 3

The 8 Levers of Change
Design the Work Environment

Scene making allows you to identify the end-point behaviors that will mark a successful transformation. Those behaviors, in turn, give you a point to work back from, toward the present. How can I redesign the work environment to bring these imagined behaviors and actions to real life? What combination of factors will make those nurses and doctors smile as the patient is being handed off from one hospital department to another? What current behaviors and practices need to be altered to get there? Is that even possible? The specificity (and accuracy) of answers to these questions turns in no small part on the level of detail in the scene you have created.

Going so deep into the weeds can often feel overly tactical or detailed, inappropriate for senior executives. But such specificity grounds the consideration of company-wide change in the experience of organizational members, the people with whom and by whom the transformation will live or die.

Actually changing what people do at work requires changing the cues they receive from their work environment—cues they receive all day, every day, whether a leader of any stripe stands in front of them or not. Otherwise, even the best-intentioned behavioral modeling or inspirational address becomes a curious non sequitur at best. As Confucius said, "The relation between superiors and inferiors is like that between the wind and the grass. The grass must bend when the wind blows across it."[1] The wind, though, can blow only so long before it must move on—and what then? Then the previous environment returns, the old cues are honored, and the grass straightens once again, unchanged by all the power and bluster that passed over it.

So, what comprises people's environment at work? Our collective six decades of experience have taught us that the work system as a whole is composed of eight environmental aspects ranging from the physical setting to available skills to rewards. Because each provides powerful cues to organizational members about how to act, each can become a powerful lever of change, a way to create the behaviors that will drive desired transformations deep into the enterprise. We describe the 8 Levers of Change in this chapter and provide multiple examples of them in use in the next.

First, an introduction to the 8 Levers of Change:

Lever	Definition
1. Organization	Structure (vertical chain of command and horizontal means of interconnection); the organizational chart; also task forces, project groups, and committees
2. Workplace design	Layout of physical and virtual space; also available work tools and technology
3. Task	Work processes, protocols, and pathways
4. People	Selection, skills, learning, and orientation of the focal organizational, business unit, department, or work unit members
5. Rewards	Rewards and punishments of every sort germane to the desired behavior or scene; compensation; intrinsic and extrinsic rewards
6. Measurement	Metrics; scorecard of performance
7. Information distribution	Who knows what, when, and how
8. Decision allocation	Who participates when, in what way, in which decisions

Lever 1: Organization

For most of us, most of the time, "organization" conjures up little more than lines and boxes on a chart. Organization is more than that, and how an organization is organized, in fact, sends off a constant stream of cues about what is expected and how to behave. Does an organization structure by geography, function/ discipline, service/product line, market segment, or information flow? What is centralized and what is decentralized? Does the organization use a matrix structure? How about the number and nature of scheduled meetings? Who attends them? What's the purpose or charter of designated groups such as staffs or cross-functional teams? All these sub-elements have a direct effect on the work environment, and all of them are potential change implementers or inhibitors.

Questions to consider when thinking about Lever 1: Organization:

- How might you change the organizational chart, including adding or subtracting positions or changing where positions report in the organization?
- How tight a coupling do you want between which groups or roles? Who is "bound" together or split apart by the formal organization as it now exists?
- What extent of horizontal integration needs structural support and where? For example, where might a matrix structure fit?
- What role might temporary or project teams play?
- What meetings or meeting systems should change? Should group charters or membership change? Which meetings should stop occurring?

Lever 2: Workplace Design

The arrangement of the physical or virtual work area; tools, supplies, and machinery, including technology and access to it; how closely (or distantly) people work together—these make up the hum of daily work life, and sometimes the Sturm und

Drang of it, too. Relatively small changes to workplace design can facilitate the larger, more global change desired.

In assessing whether Workplace Design helps or hinders interaction, we typically ask if people have access to batch email, social network software, and/or videoconferencing. Proximity matters in human behavior, in both the physical and virtual domains. The closer that people are to one another, the more likely they are to interact. Whether or not we are office friends, if we share the same coffee maker, copier, and lavatory, we *will* interact with one another.

There's more, though, and it goes back once again to the very social nature of *Homo sapiens*. Some researchers suggest that we may have developed the whites of our eyes (an unusual attribute) in order to facilitate social interaction, since the whites help us to indicate and perceive key aspects of social interaction (focus, interest, and attention) without saying a word.[2] The more workers interact, the easier it becomes for them to use this distinct social perception to gain emotional intelligence about a given set of colleagues. Breadth of interaction helps, too. One-dimensional interaction simply can never equal 3-D. Or speaking virtually, videoconferencing will increase my sense of you and how to work with you far better than will batch emails, but neither one equals sharing an office for us hardwired social animals.

Questions to consider when thinking about Lever 2: Workplace Design:

- Where might you locate people to facilitate the desired behavioral change? Do you want to recommend changes that involve people's location (who works in close proximity to whom)? How might changes to the physical space promote ease of access, collaboration, or general interaction?

- How might changes to the virtual or telephonic space ease access, collaboration, or general interaction? What role does—or might—social media, videoconferencing, or cell phone apps play?
- What tools would people need to enact the change?
- How might changes in technology affect how people perform their jobs?

Lever 3: Task

Pulling the Task Lever to create a new behavior can involve as simple an act as making a checklist of all the things that need doing, or it might involve creating a standardized process. The tools of process reengineering, "lean" manufacturing, and Total Quality Management (TQM) fit here as well. Laying out the flow of work *and* converting it into a formal practice can make it a habit—the way we do what we do.

Questions to consider when thinking about Lever 3: Task:

- What kind of work process changes does the desired end state require?
- How would the flow of the work need to change?
- Would it help to make more tasks, especially key processes, more explicit?
- Would more standardization of any processes help? Would less?

• Might the use of a particular technique such as Six Sigma aid in clarifying current and desired work processes?

Lever 4: People

Of all the Change Levers, none holds a more outsize place in the mythology of organizational change than People. The People Lever dominates our view of organizations as well as our assumptions about how to change them. Witness common expressions such as "We just don't have the right people on the bus" or "I'm playing with a B team." When a leader thinks this way, the answer is simple: replace the individuals or retool them through training or coaching, and you'll change the entire enterprise.

The point here is not to ignore hiring/firing or selection; training and development; or coaching when trying to change organizational behavior. A leader would do so at unnecessary hazard. But leaders would also do well to keep in mind Abraham Maslow's famous saying "If the only tool you have is a hammer, you tend to see every problem as a nail."[3] Over and over.

We return to a point made in the introduction, namely that much of what we attribute to the failure of individuals stems from poorly designed systems of work—that is, predictable and repeated individual failure rates by individual after individual indicate flawed systems, not necessarily flawed individuals. However you express it, though, the human and organizational costs associated with repeatedly hiring and firing individuals seldom end until leadership reworks the production process itself. W. Edwards Deming particularly stressed this point, one resembling what Stanford research psychologist Lee Ross terms "fundamental attribution error"—namely, that we erroneously attribute people's behavior to the way they are rather than to the situation they are in.[4]

Let us repeat: Getting the people element right counts, but if you attend to it without also changing other elements, you will more than likely doom the change (and the people) to failure. The "new" people (hired or trained or retrained) will step into an "old" environment and very quickly come to resemble strongly the "old" people who formerly lived in and were shaped by the same forces.

Questions to consider when thinking about Lever 4: People:

- What would the desired end state require of whom? Think particularly about which skills which people or sets of people would have to master.
- Which people or sets of people should manifest which values or orientation toward work, colleagues, customers, or other stakeholders?
- What changes in approaches to personnel practices such as hiring, reassigning, releasing, and training of personnel would facilitate enacting the desired change? What skill sets would these changes require and of whom?

Lever 5: Rewards

The word *rewards* sounds positive, but the Rewards Lever works both ways. In work life as in childhood and every other aspect of life, bad behavior is rewarded with punishment just as good behavior is rewarded with praise. What happens (if anything) to people when they act this way rather than that way, if they adopt the change or they don't? What does the organization truly recognize, ignore, reward, and punish? Obviously, money fits in here, but so do other forms of rewards (and punishment): intrinsic, social, recognition, and access (or no access) to resources and to power.

In many workplaces, rewards stand at odds with one another as well as with other Change Levers. Money may, for example, go to the highest individual performer, while social rewards go to the best-performing team. Or training may not develop skills that the enterprise rewards. Change Levers that are pulled in opposite directions conflict, generating competing sound waves that can cancel one another out.

Questions to consider when thinking about Lever 5: Rewards:

- What needs rewarding? What processes and what outcomes? What behaviors, practices, and scenes?
- What financial rewards would facilitate change? Think in terms of both what rewards (e.g., bonuses) as well as their timing and structure.
- What nonfinancial rewards would facilitate change? Think in terms of both intrinsic rewards (e.g., rewards derived from successfully completing a task) and extrinsic rewards (e.g., public recognition of accomplishment).
- What unintended consequences of your considered changes in rewards might arise? *Homo sapiens* quickly divine ways to garner valued rewards, and this can produce weirdly creative and unintended consequences.

Lever 6: Measurement

The axioms quickly pile up around the Measurement Lever: "You can't manage what you can't measure," "You treasure what you measure (or measure what you treasure)," and Deming's much-quoted "In God we trust; all others bring data."[5] The sayings promote a similar message: You cannot manage yourself or others optimally or even well if you cannot measure outcomes or results. True enough, and one good reason almost every organization develops some type of measurement standard.

But we too easily forget that measurement is also a form of communication. It tells employees on an ongoing basis what management considers important (and, by implication, not very important)—a message reinforced by the rewards that flow from high positive measurements or are denied by low ones. Align measurement with desired outcome, and good things happen. Misalign them, and an organization ends up pulling against itself.

Questions to consider when thinking about Lever 6: Measurement:

- What measures would foster and support the desired scene?
- What measures would help people to judge appropriately and accurately how they are doing?
- What metrics would help you and others manage and succeed in the new world?
- How might those measures differ from current measures?
- Should the measures focus on outcomes, process, or a combination of both?

- Do methods such as the behavioral scorecard or balanced scorecard apply?

Lever 7: Information Distribution

More than any other single factor, the flow of information determines the quality of decision making. The greater the flow and the stronger the current, the timelier and more on point decisions are likely to be. Information Distribution also has important implications for individual performance. Employees, for example, should receive performance feedback as close to instantaneously as possible. How else are they to know what actions and behaviors they need to improve?

Questions to consider when thinking about Lever 7: Information Distribution:

- What kinds of information would facilitate the occurrence of the desired behavior?
- Who needs to know what, when, in order to make the desired scenes happen?
- Who has access to performance metrics, and when?
- How real-time should the information be?
- How much information of what type should the system push out (e.g., reports) and how easily should organization members be able pull it out as needed (e.g., digital files posted on an Intranet site)?

Lever 8: Decision Allocation

Where employees fit in the process of decision making can powerfully affect their behavior. What's more, Decision Allocation cuts broadly across an enterprise, since it particularly affects and is affected by Task, Organization, and Information Distribution. Lack of alignment of these three Change Levers yields mixed signals, confusion, and frustration, and greatly enhances the likelihood that even a much-needed change initiative will fail.

Questions to consider when thinking about Lever 8: Decision Allocation:

- How would people relate to one another when performing key pieces of work or when making key decisions? For example, who leads and who follows at what point in the decision-making process?
- Who would have what type of input into which decisions and when? Who has the last word, who consults, who needs informing? Who takes the lead in spotting or attending to a given type of issue, opportunity, challenge, or initiative?
- Would formal review of decision allocation help, perhaps using a technique such as RACI charting (Responsible, Accountable, Consulted, Informed, from the Responsibility Assignment Matrix)?[6]
- How does all this fit with your thoughts about Organization, Workplace Design, and Task?

How Much to Change

Moving any one of these 8 Levers of Change will alter the work environment in specific ways and send a different set of cues to those who inhabit that environment. But how much of the environment needs to change in order to align behavior broadly with desired organizational change? The flippant answer: enough. Ideally, future research will answer this question precisely, along with questions about weighting given levers for given types of changes, or how much which levers complement one another. For now, the answer comes down to this: change enough levers enough for the owners of the behavior to perceive that the time has come to adapt to a new set of environmental cues, indeed to what qualifies as a new environment. In our best judgment, that means significantly altering at least four of the 8 Levers of Change.

Putting It All Together: The Work Systems Model

Thus far, we have advocated two tenets of change: focus on behavior and think environment. In the previous chapter, we presented an approach to envision the change you wish to see. This chapter has described eight aspects of the work environment that a change leader can use as levers to create and sustain the desired scenes—and thus the desired change. The following model provides a visual summary. Behavior sits in the midst of eight systems that comprise the overall work environment. We refer to this model as the Work Systems Model.

Figure 1: The Work Systems Model

Check Your Work, Adjust Your Work... Repeatedly

Scene (or scenes) in hand, step back. Treat your scene or scenes not as dictates, but rather as descriptions of the desired end states and use them to analyze how to craft an appropriate work environment. How should the work environment, as portrayed in the Work Systems Model, change to drive occurrence of the scenes? Carefully examine the levers of change and plan to change as many of them as much as possible in ways that will foster your scenes occurring regularly and predictably. Ask yourself if the changes in the Work Systems qualify as consistent, ideally complementary. If so, then concentrate on identifying the necessary changes in the work environment. If not, then perhaps you have unearthed inconsistencies in the conceptualization of the desired change, inconsistencies that need addressing. Better now than later. Adjust the scenes or the portfolio of scenes as necessary. Return to this process as your change effort unfolds, checking and rechecking for alignment and leverage.

In the next chapter, we present examples of successful organizational change, in which four or more Change Levers have been pulled to significantly realign the environment.

CHAPTER 4

It's Not Just One and Done
The Work Systems Model in Action

Scene creation, end-point envisioning, a thorough under-standing of the work environment and its component parts—these are all invaluable to the process of driving meaningful change deep into the enterprise. But details matter here so change leaders need to dig in and dig down. How must *your* work environment change to bring to reality the outcomes you have been envisioning? And how are you going to make that happen?

The stories in this chapter show the Work Systems Model in action. They come from a variety of industries over several decades, present change leaders from different organizational levels, and illustrate multiple types of change, but they all share one critical characteristic: success. They also illustrate an approach to change consistent with the one advocated in this book: clarity of intent and significant, coordinated alteration of at least four aspects of the work environment for those people who need to change. Whether or not they consciously pulled the levers of change, the leaders here clearly understood that until you change behavior, you have really changed nothing at all.

They also clearly understood the need to alter the environment significantly in order to alter behavior.

The message: *You can do this.*

The caveat: Like many things worth doing, embedding change in the enterprise takes time, patience, persistence, and a clear knowledge of where you want to be when the transition is complete.

Introduction of New Technology at Lloyd's of London

Seldom does capitalizing on new technology involve merely installing the technology. Rather, it involves securing changed behaviors that utilize the new technology. Lloyd's provides a case in point.

When Richard Ward became CEO of Lloyd's of London in April of 2006, he inherited a way of processing claims that dated back to the founding of the specialty insurance market a few years before the Salem witch trials began in Colonial Massachusetts. "I joined a Lloyd's that had not really changed its working practices or business practices and responded to technology in the past 320 years," Ward explained.[1] This prestigious global insurer still processed claims mainly by hand, using massive paper documentation. In fact, Lloyd's transported four tons of paper every day from London to its back-office processing center 50 miles away.

Ward envisioned a very different way of doing business at Lloyd's, one that would necessitate large-scale behavioral changes. In this new world, Lloyd's claims adjusters, lawyers, and even claimants themselves could check on the status of a claim, similar to the way one might track a FedEx or UPS package online. The envisioned scenes had multiple parties, including customers, accessing online information either on their own or by phoning a Lloyd's adjuster. In any case, key players in the Lloyd's world could procure the answers to specific questions almost immediately.

In early 2007, Ward and his team introduced an efficient electronic claims processing procedure, one that introduced a new tool (the computer) and a new process (pulling the Workplace Design and Task levers). Ward recruited "early adopters" from Lloyd's members to test out the system.[2] His goal was to have 90% of Lloyd's claims processing done electronically by the end of the year. But after initial success, the change effort stalled—stuck in implementation limbo. "We started to plateau," Ward said, "That's not unusual in a change program." Ward found himself with only about 30% of the claims being processed electronically. Many members "didn't want to change their very traditional business practices," according to Ward.[3] The old way of doing things, as slow as it was, worked well enough, and its familiarity had its own appeal. Restated, the whole work system needed to run faster and more transparently and the change was not taking hold. The key, as with most new technology adoptions, did not lie in focusing on the technical system. It lay in focusing on changing human behavior.

Lloyd's needed bigger change. The work environment needed to change more to precipitate key sets of players changing more, adapting more, and adopting the desired behavioral changes. In short, Ward needed to pull harder on more Change Levers.

To accomplish that, he and his team created a list of the top 10 performers using the new system and released it throughout the Lloyd's market. In effect, he pulled the Measurement, Information Distribution, and Rewards levers. Remembering who we are—namely, social animals—helped to predict what happened next. We tend to care, often a lot, about how others view us, and in competitive settings (such as markets), we tend to care a lot about how we compare, and how others see us compared, with competitors. The day he released the first list, Ward recalls, he got 45 complaints from people who weren't on it. "The numbers improved 15% literally overnight," he recalled. "It had quite a dramatic impact."[4]

Ward kept pulling levers. He pulled harder on the Rewards Lever by creating a powerful financial incentive: Those underwriters who resisted the electronic processing system had to invest more capital to cover their underwriting risks. Ward also set out to pull the People Lever by altering employees' orientation to and understanding of the changed work environment. He personally traveled to meet with the CEOs of all Lloyd's member companies. This kind of communication "road show" rarely succeeds by itself, but in this instance, it made a significant difference because the other changes in the work systems gave credibility to Ward's words.

By the end of 2007, Lloyd's had met its ambitious goal and was processing 90% of its claims electronically. Technology was doing its job, but only because changed behavior was allowing it to.

Creating a Culture of Innovation at Whirlpool

This case demonstrates success in dealing with three common and often overwhelming challenges for change initiators: altering culture, creating innovation, and changing when not faced with a crisis.

In 1998 the executive committee of the Whirlpool Corporation unveiled a new direction for the company, a strategy called "Brand-Focused Value Creation." David Whitwam, chairman and CEO since 1987, reflected on the daunting nature of this type of organizational change: "This is my third time trying with brands. I tried brands in 1987 when I became Chairman....The company resisted. In the early 1990s we tried the Dominant Consumer Franchise initiative. That didn't work effectively, either. So this is the third attempt, and probably my last. You see, this is a manufacturing- and engineering-oriented organization. The power base has traditionally been on the operations side, not the marketing side." In short, he believed this change important and he knew all too well its challenges.

Whirlpool was the world's largest appliance maker and did not face an immediate crisis. Whitwam, though, was taking a longer view. "As we look to the future, we realize that this is going to be a very different, very tough industry. Many people in the company think, 'The only way you can drive change is out of crisis.' There is no crisis at this time. There is no burning platform. But I've always felt you can drive change if you paint a picture of a better tomorrow."[5]

Whitwam envisioned a fundamental, strategic shift. He wanted Whirlpool to become the industry's innovation leader. To get there, it would have to develop a completely new set of organizational capabilities. Restated, Whirlpool employees at every level would have to behave very differently.

Historically, Whirlpool relied on just two groups, engineering and marketing, to generate all the company's new product ideas. These two groups "owned" innovation and divided it between them. Whitwam envisioned an organization in which everyone owned innovation and everyone focused on it. He enlisted the help of Nancy Snyder, then corporate director of the organization and leadership change process, to create an implementation plan that would spread innovation companywide, soliciting ideas from all of Whirlpool's 61,000 employees so that innovation would "generate from everywhere and everyone."[6] He also employed Gary Hamel and his consulting firm, Strategos.

Whitwam and Snyder pulled nearly all the levers to change the culture at Whirlpool. They introduced new metrics and created criteria for innovation projects, setting annual revenue goals coming from innovation. By 2006 the company hit its $1 billion revenue goal. Whitwam and Snyder also began tracking how many ideas came in, how long it took an idea to go through the pipeline, and what happened to it (Measurement). The resource allocation process was also changed to reflect the emphasis on innovation (Task and Decision Allocation levers). In 2001, divisions needed to deploy 10% of their capital investment dollars to innovation projects in order to receive their full allocation of capital. The following year, the required percentage of capital rose to 20%.

Whirlpool pulled the Rewards Lever by tying annual performance reviews to short- and long-term success at meeting those goals and to the quality of the business plans and implementation work that went with them. For senior executives, a third of their pay was linked directly to what came out of the innovation pipeline. For rank-and-file employees, the rewards were team-based and not financial. "The reward," Snyder explained, "is recognition by your peers." She also said that the innovation challenge excited Whirlpool employees. "We had no idea how motivating this would be….People at the bottom were saying, 'Finally someone gets it!'"[7]

Eliciting lots of fresh ideas provided only a start. As Snyder put it, "Our CEO would go out and talk to thousands of people and say, 'We are going to have innovation from everywhere and everyone. If you have a concept, put it forward.' But we didn't have the systems in place to react to this."[8]

Clearly, a number of the Work Systems needed changing in order to support and develop the desired patterns of behavioral change this new strategy required. So Whirlpool pulled the People Lever and trained nearly 600 "I-mentors"—the I stands for innovation—whom Snyder described as being "like Six Sigma black belts. They had real jobs, but they also had special training in how to facilitate innovation projects and help people with their ideas. It's very likely that in your location or the department next to you, there's an I-mentor who you can talk to."[9] These I-mentors trained other employees, ensured the quality of projects, and accelerated the progress of project implementation. Creating this special function and offering a process for innovating meant that Whirlpool was pulling the Organization and Task levers in addition to the People Lever. By 2005, all employees were completing training in order to receive basic proficiency certification in innovation.[10]

To pull the Workplace Design and Information Distribution levers, Snyder's team created a suite of online resources called the Innovation E-Space.[11] This tool allows people to develop a business idea, win resources for it, contact innovation mentors, and share ideas with other employees.

Prior to the change, Whirlpool's extremely conservative budget-control process had helped contain costs but tended to strangle new ideas. Like most organizations, Whirlpool budgeted annually, and once complete, its budget changed little if at all. Thus, if someone came up with a great new idea after completion of the budget, no money existed to fund it. More flexible funding was needed to support more flexible, innovative thinking, so Whirlpool reworked the budgeting process (Task) and Decision Allocation. Whitwam had each region set up a seed fund for innovation and told the senior team that they had to fund all the ideas that came forward, no exceptions. Whitwam also set up his own separate seed fund. He told employees, "If any innovator goes to their regional innovation head with an idea that the SBU head will not fund, they can come to me."[12]

As Whitwam pressed these changes, Whirlpool's senior leadership resisted. To break that logjam, he put executives through an "innovations champion program" and assigned senior leaders as sponsors for innovation projects (People and Decision Allocation). Whirlpool also set up I-Boards throughout the company, with responsibility for nurturing and funding innovation ideas (Organization and Decision Allocation). Finally, by creating the seed funds and freeing them from the traditional budget cycle, Whirlpool placed authority over this funding in the hands of those lower down the organizational ladder—another big change in Decision Allocation.

Without a crisis, Whirlpool pulled all 8 Levers of Change and successfully embedded innovation into its culture. Its "innovation pipeline" went from $1.3 billion to $3.3 billion in 2006.[13] Seven years after launch, Whirlpool's share price stood at an all-time high, and the company posted record results. Much of that growth was fueled by new, innovative items commanding premium prices.

Really Big Change: TechnoServe and Industry-Level Change

What about applications of the approach advocated in this book to even larger canvases? What if, for instance, one wanted to create economic growth in a poverty-stricken African nation such as Mozambique?

Ed Bullard, a Connecticut businessman, founded Techno-Serve in 1968 to apply private-sector tools to help people in developing nations. Today, TechnoServe focuses on developing entrepreneurs, building businesses and industries, and improving the business environment in more than 40 countries around the world.[14] In 2004, it began working with consultants McKinsey & Company to transform the poultry industry in destitute Mozambique. At the time, Mozambique imported most of its chickens for sale from Brazil for a simple reason: price. Brazilian chickens cost less than locally raised chickens because of the inefficiencies in Mozambique's poultry industry. Brazilians froze their chickens, shipped them through the Middle East, and still beat the price of Mozambican chickens. However, the Brazilian chickens took so long to get to Mozambique that often they appeared at market past their sell-by date. Furthermore, Mozambique's inefficiencies meant fewer jobs in a country desperately in need of jobs, income, and greater economic health.

Envisioning a different future entailed considerable data collection, including hundreds of interviews. Barriers were many and interrelated: a lack of locally available feed, few successful entrepreneurs operating hatcheries, few quality or sanitation standards, no industry organization, and no retail marketing. To succeed, TechnoServe and its partners would need to create "targeted, time-limited and integrated interventions across the value chain to catalyze longer-term industry growth."[15] To get there, TechnoServe and its partners would not only have to pull almost every Change Lever and do so nearly simultaneously.

TechnoServe pulled the People Lever by providing training for smallholder poultry farmers and helped them improve their production practices (the People and Task levers at work). It upgraded processing equipment to expand production capacity (Workplace Design and Task levers). The government organized a trade group, the Mozambican Aviculture Association, which created an AMA seal to ensure high quality (the Organization and Measurement levers). The AMA also launched a multimedia campaign throughout the country to promote the consumption of locally produced poultry and the new safety standards (Information Distribution). The government worked with Cargill, Michigan State University, and the University of Minnesota to introduce biosecurity measures for food safety (the Task and Measurement levers).

By 2009, within five years of launch, the Mozambican poultry industry had grown more than fourfold. Local chicken consumption rose to 76% of the total market. And the estimated boost for the country's GDP totaled a robust 5%.[16]

Change from the Bottom Up

A shop floor supervisor from one of Greg's client organizations approached Greg during a break in a class and asked for a minute to talk.[17] Greg did not recall having ever met the man—let's call him Joe—but quickly agreed. Joe had taken a workshop based on the Work Systems Model and proceeded to walk Greg through a set of changes he had initiated based on the model. Basically, he sought to have Greg "check his work."

In a unionized setting, the supervisor had come up with a vision of creating regular, ongoing, efficiency-improving and problem-solving meetings with his direct reports. He tackled Workplace Design by finding a flip chart, a table, and a few chairs, and clearing a small space on the shop floor. He developed a protocol and clarified decision-making authority with his own management hierarchy and that of the union. Then he selected a few workers and trained them a bit himself on basic process reengineering tools and gathered them in regular meetings.

Joe figured the rewards of improving operations would count for something, as would the paid time off, and he chipped in out of his own pocket for a few T-shirts. As for Measurement, he devised and calculated a few metrics and hand-posted them on a board in the unit. He reported that all seemed to be progressing well, but he wanted to know what Greg thought about his efforts and what he might do to improve his chances for success.

Greg's response: "Well, first off and most important, you're definitely working above your pay grade." But Joe, of course, had done far more than that. The foreman had cobbled together a comprehensive approach to creating a new behavior pattern in his unit in order to increase its performance. He had pushed all

8 Levers of Change despite a modest span of control and limited resources. He also got to envision a dream and make it a reality.

Sustaining Customer Service at Disney

Many people have "gone to school" on Disney's theme parks in the hope of changing their organizations. They come to study how it produces and sustains remarkable levels of customer satisfaction. Small wonder, since currently Disney boasts a 70% customer return rate. Indeed, so many companies came to ask for customer service advice from Disney that the company started the Disney Institute, a consulting business focused on improving customer service. The Disney Institute has doubled its revenues over the past three years and counts among its customers a wide array of international and national organizations, ranging from United Airlines to 300 different school systems to the organizers of the 2012 Super Bowl.[18] Disney's great secret? Precisely what we have been writing about here: constructing scenes and designing work environments in order to generate and sustain desired behaviors.

Disney's vision is exceptional customer service. To create scenes, it borrows a technique from the motion picture industry: storyboarding. Disney designers create a three-dimensional world by seeing it first in two dimensions, as a storyboard, to "map the experience from a guest's perspective and improve and troubleshoot the proposed action before it ever gets off the storyboard." Disney creates the scene and then uses it to identify how to design its work systems to create the envisioned ideal customer experience—the "magic"—for guests to its theme parks.[19]

Disney employs many of the tools associated with the People Lever, such as a rigorous selection process and extensive orientation and training. It also pulls the Task and Measurement levers by setting and holding to rigid standards for how its employees look. Disney pulls harder on the Task Lever by defining the way employees do every aspect of their work, sometimes down to the smallest detail. For example, "one of the first things Disney employees [who direct guests at the theme parks] are taught is how to point courteously,"[20] with two fingers or an open hand, because of the impoliteness attributed in some cultures to pointing with one finger. As for scripting, Disney has invented an entire lexicon, one that designates employees as "cast members," customers as "guests," and rides as "attractions."

Disney continually works to improve Workplace Design. It studies and measures its guests and their behavior extensively and then uses that data to improve customer experience. No data, no change, seems too small. Consider the distance between trash cans. Disney discovered through study that customers, on average, traveled 27 paces with a candy wrapper before discarding it; hence, Disney placed trash cans every 27 paces. Disney provides electronic sign boards informing guests of the wait time at various popular rides, thereby increasing customers' or "guests'" ability to plan their day (Information Distribution and Decision Allocation). Founder Walt Disney's emphasis on setting (Workplace Design) lives on in the company motto: "Everything speaks."[21] Walt even mandated changing the texture of the pavement as guests moved from one area of the park to another. He insisted, "You can get information about a changing environment through the soles of your feet."[22]

Consider but one customer service scene: tired guests who have forgotten where in Epcot's expansive parking lot they parked their car. Tram drivers could help the weary guests find that car because the drivers started keeping a list of which row in a lot was filled at which time of day (Task). The information from that process went to parking employees at the end of the day (Information Distribution), allowing them to direct a family to the right parking row just by asking what time the family arrived at the park. The information allows the employee confidently to respond or even to take the initiative by asking if they can help. They make the choice (Decision Allocation), and in doing so, they draw upon both information and training (Task, People).

Decision Allocation at Disney blends tightly scripted encounters and considerable discretion in order to provide customers with a predictably high level of service as well as the most pleasant (and appreciated) of service surprises. In "Disney Service Basics," Jeff Kober explains, "The typical tendency for leaders is to try and map out all of the possible behaviors their employees should demonstrate when working with customers. This approach is flawed....First, such behaviors come across as rote, rather than genuine."[23] Hence, Disney uses the Decision Allocation Lever to foster exemplary service by encouraging employees to do something that we know gives most of us intrinsic pleasure: namely, aiding others. A Disney program called Take 5 encourages employees to take five minutes to individualize customer service by doing something nice for customers: giving a gift, leaving their post to take a photo for a customer (often of a customer), or replacing a fallen ice cream cone. Such initiative breaks up the employee's routine and energizes him, but more important, it can lead to this scene: a frazzled, worried, and disappointed family retreats to its room lugging a sick child and finds, to everyone's delight, a personalized get-well card from no less than Mickey Mouse.

Sustained, predictably great service comes from a comprehensive systems approach. "Companies come in and say, 'Just make my employees smile more,'" says Jeff James, who runs Disney's consulting arm, "but you can't take Disney and just plug it in."[24] As we've said repeatedly, to bring about and sustain desired behavior you have to envision, create scenes, and pull multiple levers in the Work Systems Model. That's hard work, but the reward is great.

In Summary

Change often fails not because people lack the capacity to change but because the work environment does not change in ways that encourage people to employ their adaptive capacity to change. Perhaps the greatest benefit of the Work Systems Model comes down to reminding the change leader to focus on behavior and to think environment. Envision the behavior and alter the environment accordingly, as broadly and as deeply as possible. Both the success and the variety of the cases just presented bear witness to the power of this approach.

CHAPTER 5

When to Use
the Work Systems Model

The previous chapter presented examples of how the Work Systems Model looks in action. Here we concentrate on when to apply it.

Discipline for Change Initiatives

If leaders ignore behavior as the critical issue, even radical transformations can begin to look deceptively (even dangerously) easy. The danger of such miscalculation is real. Consider the following image. Greg's father managed in a company that fabricated and erected steel, usually in bridges and buildings. Workers regularly toiled at considerable heights to install huge steel beams that dwarfed the workers in size and weight. Cranes hoisted the beams, which swayed as the result of a confluence of forces. The swaying could have a slow, rhythmic quality to it, belying the power of its causes. Occasionally, a worker grew frustrated with the time and effort it took to get a beam into place, and he would reach out a hand in the sadly mistaken belief that he might easily stop the beam's seemingly gentle swaying and make it comply. Predictably, the worker suffered the rudest of awakenings to the power of physical forces at play as the beam launched him into the air. He received the most unforgettable of lessons—if he survived the teaching.

So it is with organizational change. A multitude of cues determines what employees do and don't do, whether they adapt or hold tight to old ways. Inevitably, the behavior of employees reflects the confluence of powerful forces. Aligning those forces through thoughtful application of the 8 Levers of Change in the Work Systems Model will precipitate behavioral change. Not doing so can well lead to an unforgettable lesson in how not to approach leading an organization through change.

The Work Systems Model (and associated tenets) help guide and discipline the implementation of organizational change. Constructing and editing scenes, for example, pushes far more detailed consideration of a change, of what it is and of what it is not. Maybe your response to the scene will be "That's what we want middle managers to be doing!" Or perhaps "Is that what we want middle managers to be doing?" and you'll have to go back and think through the scene again. Either way, the process leads naturally to a second set of considerations: "Why do people predictably and frustratingly not do what we say we want them to do? Let's go lever by lever to discern what messages we are actually sending about what we want." The Work Systems Model takes time and effort, precisely because organizational behavior can prove so complex, but few things waste as much time and effort as a failed change initiative. Disciplined design of change is time well spent.

Lastly, returning to the model throughout a change initiative provides ongoing discipline for refining and advancing as you go along.

Deciding to Proceed with a Change Initiative or Not

Perhaps the most difficult decision that confronts many change leaders comes down to "pursue the change or not." The Work Systems Model is invaluable here as well. If you cannot change the equivalent of four Change Levers significantly, then don't bother. Stop and try something else. If someone else wishes to pursue such a change, then use the Work Systems Model to help them make the "go/no go" choice. Share the model or at least its logic. Ideas for change initiatives abound, but someone has to know when to open and when to turn off the spigot.

Commitment to Change

Commitment to change seldom comes easily to most of us. Even people with serious heart disease often struggle mightily with committing to change despite the high stakes involved, including quality of life and mortality itself. "If you look at people after coronary-artery bypass grafting two years later, 90% of them have not changed their lifestyle," said Dr. Edward Miller, former dean of the medical school and CEO of the hospital at Johns Hopkins. "And that's been studied over and over and over again....Even though they know they have a very bad disease and they know they should change their lifestyle, for whatever reason, they can't."[1]

By contrast, 77% of the patients who enroll in Dean Ornish's heart program succeed. Ornish believes that people often find radical, comprehensive, sweeping changes easier than small, incremental ones. This is so partly because patients who go on the "tough, radical" and comprehensive Ornish program see much quicker results than those who try, and largely fail, to make more incremental change. In Ornish's program, patients report a 91% decrease in the frequency of chest pain in the first month.

"These rapid improvements are a powerful motivator," Ornish says. "When people who have had so much chest pain that they can't work, or make love, or even walk across the street without intense suffering find that they are able to do all of those things without pain in only a few weeks, then they often say, 'These are choices worth making.'"[2] The very intense Ornish program encourages personal commitment because, by tangibly improving their lives, it makes sense to the participants.

Likewise, meaningful organizational change needs leaders to demonstrate their commitment, and to enable early success by those who attempt change. People need both because they harbor understandable and justifiable skepticism about change initiatives. They know the data about the rate of failure of organizational change efforts even if they have not read the studies. Failed change has burned them before. Before jumping aboard, people look for signs of fortitude from leadership. Their commitment also turns on the changes making sense to them within their environment. Consider the relative power of two demonstrations of commitment.

One leader visits every location, announcing and stressing the need for increased standardization of processes to drive cost down and quality up. A second leader makes no visits or speeches. Members of the organization, however, cannot help but notice a set of aligned changes in their work environment: a new organization chart; alteration of workspace design in conjunction with delineation of standard work processes; a schedule for training in lean manufacturing; reward and recognition programs based on new measurements of standardization, cost, and quality; enhanced access to data on cost, quality, and variation; and altered decision allocation along work processes rather than within traditional silos.

By making meaningful shifts in the workplace environment, the second leader has more powerfully demonstrated commitment to the change. This leader "went first," setting the stage for early successes by organizational members who adapt to the new environment. These early adapters, in turn, will do better faster, and their commitment to the change will grow. A virtuous circle all around.

Sustainable Change

Many a change leader has bemoaned the temporary nature of many an organizational change. A concerted push and massing of attention gets the proverbial ball rolling—but not for long. If a temporary change is the aim, then such a fade does not matter, and certainly no change will last forever. As Plato wrote, "All is flux, nothing stays still."[3] However, most change leaders seek to establish significant change efforts solidly enough that they will endure, prove self-sustaining, and require a concerted effort to undo.

Building a work environment that supports desired change helps both to launch the change and to secure it. Recall Disney. Coordinating Change Levers not only supports changing behavior but serves to secure it by making the desired behavior make more sense than other behaviors. Hence, as long as the levers stay in place, so, too, should the desired change, and that equals sustainable change.

The Connective Tissue
That Gets Strategy Implemented

Book after book, article after article, presents approaches to strategy. The continued outpouring of this writing indicates the ongoing interest in how to devise strategy, but as Cynthia Montgomery, Harvard's Timken Professor of Business, notes, "Strategy has become more about formulation than implementation, and more about getting the analysis right at the outset than living with a strategy over time."[4] The highly checkered record of successful strategy implementation supports Montgomery's claim. A devotee of this stream of work can read long and carefully without encountering a focus on the behavioral implications of strategic choices. Yet to ignore that reality in framing and designing strategy implementation would seem at least curious and more likely dangerous.

Embracing the notion that strategic change necessitates behavioral change means doing as we have advised in this book. First, construct scenes of desired patterns of behavior in order to ground the discussion of implementation and enable clearer communication of its intent. Second, review which Change Levers will drive those behavioral changes. Use this review to guide time and resource allocation and to sharpen discussion of such pivotal strategic questions as "Can we actually pull this off?" In summary, the Work Systems Model connects the strategic intent (or wish) with the organizational realities of change, a key connection and one too often weakly made.

An Antidote to Mergers and Acquisitions Failure

Mergers and acquisitions (M&A) qualify as among the largest and costliest changes that an organization can undertake. Most underperform and many fail. Problems include hubris and the thrill of the hunt sweeping all before them, overcoming sound judgment. Applying the Work Systems Model helps to avoid an all-too-common pattern of failure. To see how, look at the 2000 union of TD Bank Financial Group with Canada Trust Financial Services, at the time the largest financial services merger in Canadian history.

This merger brought together two companies with 1,500 branches, 44,000 employees, 10 million customers, and $256 billion in assets. As with many mergers, the architects of this one sought to gain scale and to keep the best practices of each bank so that the newly formed organization could achieve its larger goal of becoming the leading Canadian-based financial institution in all of North America. As with too few mergers, though, these change leaders kept behavior (both internal and external) at the forefront of their planning.

"We were religious in our measurement of how employees were feeling," Fred Tomczyk, TD Bank's vice chair, told researchers, "and customer service was measured just as religiously and then tied to bonuses throughout the organization. The satisfaction-monitoring systems used at TD Canada Trust were deployed quickly, efficiently, and visibly, and customer satisfaction feedback was quickly given to employees....The goal is to entrench the desired behaviors and practices so deeply that they become not only routine but taken for granted."[5]

In effect, the leaders used the tenets that underlie the Work Systems Model. They avoided common traps by accurately evaluating what a true merger or large acquisition would require: operational synergies, not a portfolio play or a strip-and-flip. They focused on identifying and embedding behavior. From there, the M&A point people could consider the necessary changes in work environment, and their cost and feasibility, before embarking on the type of change initiative too often poorly imagined and disastrously hurried.

A Practical Approach to Cultural Change

Of all organizational changes, cultural change probably has the highest record of failure. According to research conducted by the Katzenbach Center at Booz & Company in 2010, between two-thirds to three-quarters of culture change efforts fail.[6] Many other studies agree. The problem is that so many cultural change initiatives have it backward.

Too often, organizations approach culture as if it existed separately from the work environment within the organization. Typically, anthropological analysis identifies norms and values; surveys and workshops produce carefully crafted lists of new, more desirable norms and values; and proselytizing ensues— along with "appropriate" reeducation interventions.

Cultural change requires altering "the way we do what we do," but leaders too often focus on the culture as if it generated the patterns of behavior, instead of the reverse. Behavior, adaptive to the environment, drives culture. No less an expert than Edgar Schein says in his fourth and latest edition of *Organizational Culture and Leadership*:

Before we even start to think about culture, we need to 1) have a clear definition of the operational problem or issue that started the change process, and to 2) formulate specific behavioral goals…it is therefore very important…to identify the actual behaviors that the client wants to change.[7]

The Work Systems Model points cultural change leaders in this different and more useful direction. If you apply the Work Systems Model, by definition, you will have changed—not because that necessarily constituted your original intent or focus but because what *defines* culture (namely, patterns of behavior) will have changed.

Conclusion

Organizations are ultimately huge, complex systems of behaviors. Therefore, leaders who focus on changing behavior markedly increase their odds of successfully changing organizations. The good news for leaders is that behaviors are, in fact, immensely malleable. Human behavior twists and shifts. Immense behavioral variations over millennia bear witness to our marvelous capacity to adapt to the changing world around us. Our ability to adapt to our environment, be it physical or virtual, still impresses. In organizations, the "environment" means the work environment, which is characterized by eight aspects. A change leader who converts those aspects into levers will significantly increase the odds for successful change.

In times like ours, times dominated by change, leaders need to design and implement organizational change from the ground up. Of course, that process should encompass environmental scanning, critical analysis of markets and organizational capabilities, an understanding of psychological processes of change, careful coalition building, well-considered stakeholder management, skilled project management, and appreciation for the role of clear messaging and modeling. Those are givens, but a large piece of the change puzzle comes down to the focus of this book: Do you know what behaviors the change will require? And will those desired behaviors make sense, in the final analysis, to those who determine whether the proposed change will succeed or fail?

Let us repeat: We believe that big, radical change can actually prove easier to create and adapt to than incremental change— but only when that big change is *clear* and the works systems are *aligned*. What we too often see instead are lots of small or incremental changes, none of them bold enough to be successful, competing against one another for scarce resources in a system that is sending confusing and contradictory messages. People try to interpret the noise and end up shrugging. Doing things the "old way" is easier than trying to reconcile the competing messages.

How do you clearly align the work systems? It comes back to the two tenets we laid out in chapter 1:

1. Focus on the behaviors that you want from people.
2. Design the work environment to foster those behaviors.

The 8 Levers of Change will help you build a work environment that creates the desired behavior. But don't forget to go far enough: you must change enough of the work environment to change how people experience it. Successful change means pulling at least four of the 8 Levers of Change.

Our world—full of uncertainty, innovation, opportunity, and peril—requires much from leaders, and followers. Leaders seek to recruit disciples to drive change. Disciples often want the same. They can see the need at ground level. But followers also want and deserve something else: *a fighting chance*, and change leaders should want no less for them. As Napoleon said, "Soldiers generally win battles; generals get credit for them."[1]

Change in a large organization likely means transforming the behavior of thousands, even tens of thousands, of people spread across numerous divisions and multiple continents. With an executive's support, a disciple of change may receive attention in the boardroom, but the deeper within an organization she attempts change, the greater the importance of the local environment. And the farther from Rome (or Paris) that disciple labors, the less value the emperor's words carry.

The disciple will have to work within the total work environment of how people are actually organized; of the skills, information, and tools they have at hand; of the people with whom they interact; of the protocols and allocation of decision-making authority that guide their actions; and of the rewards or punishments that come to them based on measurement. In short, the disciple will have to deal with the work systems that comprise people's work environment, the reality that people see every day at and around their offices or work stations. This local environment shapes local behaviors. A disciple who tries to initiate change at odds with the local reality will almost certainly fail.

Telling people, for example, to concentrate on cross-unit quality when their environment tells them to concentrate on within-unit volume means promoting a change that doesn't make sense. This then generates a conflict that lessens both people's willingness to alter their behavior and, simultaneously, their tolerance for the change disciple. A change disciple who chooses to apply increasing amounts of personal pressure in the face of such a disconnect between change message and local reality, especially by employing punitive actions such as disciplining or firing, will precipitate a choice: act as the disciple wishes and have the system punish you, or act as the system wishes and have the disciple punish you. Given such a choice, the locals will tend to place the smart bet on the system and against the change disciple. They will move to marginalize, then neutralize, and if necessary eliminate the disciple.

Sending change disciples out to do hard labor without concomitant attention by leaders to work systems essentially strands those disciples. Leaders who rely on the disciple's labor but don't change the work environment adequately set up the disciples to fail. That failure costs leaders and disciples alike. Failure to change the work environment therefore amounts to a breach of fiduciary responsibility by the leadership because it leads predictably to squandered resources. Such failure also qualifies as immoral because of what it does to human beings, especially to the disciples of change.

In this book, we have offered the Work Systems Model because it has helped leaders across industries, organizational levels, and multiple decades to do well by their organizations, by the disciples of change, and thereby by themselves. We hope that you, regardless of your industry or title, find that it helps you at least as much as it helped them.

Acknowledgments

This book sits atop decades of work and the instruction and collaboration of scores of people. Many talented professionals—professors, writers, and consultants—have shaped our respective studies and learning at Harvard College, Yale University, Westinghouse, CFAR, The Coxe Group, and The Wharton School.

Cassie would particularly like to thank her colleagues at CFAR for two decades of their wisdom and partnership and Kenwyn Smith for his mentorship and inspiration.

Greg would like to thank a few additional (and treasured) fellow travelers: Rev. Robert Ginn for starting him down this path nearly 40 years ago; J. Richard Hackman for talking him into attending Yale's PhD program; Clayton Alderfer and John Low-Beer for keeping him in that program; Lady Nancy Seear and Robert Guest at the London School of Economics for leading an extraordinary 12-month master's program experience (and Rotary International for funding it!); Westinghouse coworkers for providing a true and lasting education in organizational change; John Lubin for recruiting him to Wharton; Elizabeth

Andy for so generously facilitating his first year there; John Kimberly for fostering his continued connection with Wharton; and partners at the Coxe Group for consistently demonstrating valuable and ethical management consulting.

Greg and Cassie offer a special thanks to Janice Rowland for her tireless research, organization, and project management. She invested hundreds of hours in this book and, in nearly countless very practicable ways, made it possible. We also most sincerely thank the team at Wharton Digital Press for their original interest and enduring faith in this project and their valuable contributions to the book. In particular, Steve Kobrin and Shannon Berning read and reread, critiqued, and edited our work over and over. Simply stated, they helped to make this book possible in the first instance and then better and better in scores of subsequent instances. They also connected us with another talented editor, Howard Means. Howard took the time to understand the work presented here and then helped us communicate it more powerfully.

Cassie would like to thank Carole and Joe for their unfailing belief in her and for sending her off to Yale, and Connie Alexis-Laona for a lifetime of friendship and cheerleading. She would also like to thank Bruce Gillis for his unwavering support through thick and thin and, of course, for the girls.

Greg, for his part, turns to his wife and says, "Thank you. Thank you for all of it, including tolerating my distant, lost in thought, 'much less fun' self who wandered through our home during the various bouts of actually writing this book."

Finally, Greg and Cassie each have and continue to work with dedicated, talented clients. They have shared struggles, failures, and triumphs of changing their organizations. So many looked at the central component of this book, the Work Systems Model, and said, "That's useful. Say more." That validation, that encouragement as much as anything else yielded this book. Thank you.

Notes

Introduction: Why Change Initiatives Fail

1 Gregory P. Shea, PhD, and Robert Gunther, *Your Job Survival Guide: A Manual for Thriving in Change* (Upper Saddle River, NJ: FT Press, 2009).

2 Roger G. Ackerman and Gary L. Neilson, "Partnering for Results: A Case Study of Re-engineering, the Corning Way," *Strategy + Business* (April 1, 1996), www.strategy-business.com/article/14910?pg=all (accessed September 21, 2012); Carolyn Aiken and Scott Keller, "The Irrational Side of Change Management," *McKinsey Quarterly* (April 2009), www.mckinseyquarterly.com (accessed September 21, 2012); Ronald N. Ashkenas, "Beyond the Fads: How Leaders Drive Change with Results," *Human Resource Planning* 17, no. 2 (June 1, 1994): 25–44; Philip Atkinson, "Managing Resistance to Change," *Management Services* (April 1, 2005); Hans Henrik Jørgensen, Lawrence Owen, and Andreas Neus, "Making Change Work: IBM Global Study 2008," IBM Corporation, October 14, 2008, www-935.ibm.com/services/us/gbs/bus/pdf/gbe03100-usen-03-making-change-work.pdf (accessed September 21, 2012); Pivotal Resources, "Research Finds Almost Half of Change Initiatives at U.S. Corporations Are Failing to Meet Goals," Pivotal Resources, February 5, 2008, http://67.20.105.193/about/press-releases/failing-to-meet-goals.html (accessed September 21, 2012); John Darragh and Andrew Campbell, "Why Corporate Initiatives Get Stuck," *Long Range Planning* 34, no. 1 (February 2001): 33–52; The Ken Blanchard Companies, White Paper 100208, "Leadership Strategies for Making Change Stick," 2008, www.kenblanchard.com/...Leadership/...Leadership.../leadership_strategies_ for_making_change_stick/ (accessed September 21, 2012); and Marcia W. Blenko, Michael C. Mankins, and Paul Rogers, "The Decision-Driven Organization," *Harvard Business Review* (June 2010), http://hbr.org/2010/06/the-decision-driven-organization/ar/1 (accessed September 21, 2012).

81

3 Gregory P. Shea, PhD, "Leading Change," in S. Rovin, ed., Medicine and Business, Aspen, 2001. The Work Systems Model is copyrighted by Shea and Associates, Inc.

4 Eric Trist and Ken Bamforth, "Some Social and Psychological Consequences of the Longwall Method of Coal Getting," *Human Relations 4* (1951): 3–38.

Chapter One: So, You Say You Want a Revolution?
1 Names in the Halloran case study were changed to protect identities. The information comes from interviews with Cassie Solomon and the client, 2008.

2 John Tierney, "Be It Resolved," *New York Times*, January 5, 2012, www.nytimes.com/2012/01/08/sunday-review/new-years-resolutions-stick-when-willpower-is-reinforced.html?pagewanted=all (accessed July 28, 2012); *Willpower: Rediscovering the Greatest Human Strength*, by Roy F. Baumeister and John Tierney (New York: Penguin Books, 2011).

Chapter Two: Make a Scene
1 Correspondence with Göran Carstedt, August 2012.

2 Carmen Nobel, "Are You a Strategist?" Harvard Business School Working Knowledge, July 16, 2012. http://hbswk.hbs.edu/pdf/item7022.pdf (accessed November 11, 2012).

3 The Pareto principle. Nick Bunkley, "Joseph Juran, 103, Pioneer in Quality Control, Dies," *New York Times*, March 3, 2008, www.nytimes.com/2008/03/03/business/03juran.html?_r=1 (accessed September 3, 2012).

4 Names in the ER critical care case study have been changed to protect identities. The information comes from client work and interviews conducted by Cassie Solomon, 2011.

Chapter Three: The 8 Levers of Change
1 James Legge, *The Chinese Classics: Life and Teachings of Confucius* (London: N. Trubner and Co, 1869), p. 197.

2 Ker Than, "Did Evolution Make Our Eyes Stand Out?" Livescience.com, November 8, 2006, www.msnbc.msn.com/id/15625720/ns/technology_and_science-science/t/did-evolution-make-our-eyes-stand-out/#.UC0_dI4lZSU (accessed September 3, 2012).

3 Ashton Applewhite, Tripp Evans, and Andrew Frothingham, "And I Quote," *The Definitive Collection of Quotes, Sayings*, rev. ed. (New York: St. Martin's Press, 2003), p. 57.

4 Lee Ross, "The Intuitive Psychologist and His Shortcomings: Distortions in the Attribution Process," in Leonard Berkowitz, ed., *Advances in Experimental Social Psychology* (New York: Academic Press, 1977), p. 184.

5 Trevor Hastie, Robert Tibshirani, and Jerome Friedman, *The Elements of Statistical Learning*, 2nd ed. (New York: Springer, 2009).

6 "RACI: Teams That Work" Whitepaper, http://www.racitraining.com/free-raci-whitepaper (accessed November 11, 2012).

Chapter Four: It's Not Just One and Done

1 Jena McGregor, "Issue: Bringing Lloyd's of London into the 21st Century," *Bloomberg Businessweek*, July 22, 2008, p. 1, www.businessweek.com/managing/content/jul2008/ca20080722_853361.htm (accessed December 27, 2010).

2 Definition of member: "Unlike many other insurance companies, Lloyd's is not a company; it's a market where our members join together as syndicates to insure risks. The Lloyd's market is home to over 50 managing agents and over 80 syndicates," www.lloyds.com/Lloyds/About-us/What-is-lloyds (accessed September 3, 2012).

3 McGregor., p. 2.

4 Ibid.

5 Jan W. Rivkin, Dorothy Leonard, and Gary Hamel, "Change at Whirlpool Corporation (A)," *Harvard Business School Publishing*, 9-705-462, rev. March 6, 2006, p. 1, www.hbsp.harvard.edu (accessed December 3, 2010).

6 Ibid., p. 1.

7 Michael Arndt, "How Whirlpool Defines Innovation," interview with Nancy Snyder by Michael Arndt, *Businessweek*, March 6, 2006, www.businessweek.com/print/innovate/content/mar2006/id20060306_287425.htm (accessed December 3, 2010).

8 Ibid., p. 2.

9 Ibid.

10 The Conference Board, "HR's Role in Building a Culture of Innovation" *Executive Action Series*, No. 159, September 2005.

11 Jan W. Rivkin, Dorothy Leonard, and Gary Hamel, "Change at Whirlpool Corporation (B)," *Harvard Business School Publishing*, 9-705-463, rev. March 6, 2006, p. 6, www.hbsp.harvard.edu (accessed December 3, 2010).

12 Ibid., p. 6.

13 Arndt, "How Whirlpool Defines Innovation," p. 1.

14 www.technoserve.org/who-we-are/our-history (accessed August 28, 2012).

15 Bruce McNamer, "Helping Africans to Jump-Start Their Industries," *McKinsey Quarterly* (June 2010): 3, www.mckinseyquarterly.com/Food_Agriculture/Helping_Africans_to_jump_start_their_industries_2596 (accessed July 10, 2012).

16 Ibid., p. 2.

17 Names in the manufacturing facility case study have been changed to protect identities. The information comes from an interview conducted by Greg Shea.

18 "In Customer Service Consulting, Disney's Small World is Growing" by Brooks Barnes, *New York Times*, April 22, 2012.

19 Disney Institute, *Be Our Guest: Perfecting the Art of Customer Service* (New York: Disney Editions, 2001), p. 183.

20 Ibid., p. 49.

21 Ibid., p. 23.

22 Ibid.

23 Jeff Kober, "Disney Service Basics," *Mouse Planet*, November 29, 2007, www.mouseplanet.com/6978/Disney_Service_Basics (accessed June 1, 2012).

24 Barnes, A-1.

Chapter Five: When to Use the Work Systems Model

1 Alan Deutschman, "Change or Die," *Fast Company*, May 1, 2005, p. 6 www.fastcompany.com/52717/change-or-die (accessed August 11, 2012).

2 Ibid.

3 Fred R. Shapiro, *The Yale Book of Quotations* (Hartford, CT: Yale University Press, 2006), p. 356.

4 Cynthia Montgomery, *The Strategist: Be the Leader Your Business Needs* (New York: HarperBusiness, 2012).

5 Thomas B. Lawrence, Bruno Dyck, Sally Maitlis, and Michael K. Mauws, "The Underlying Structure of Continuous Change," *MIT Sloan Management Review* (July 1, 2006), http://sloanreview.mit.edu/the-magazine/articles/2006/summer/47412/the-underlying-structure-of-continuous-change/ (accessed December 13, 2010).

6 Ian W. Rivkin, Dorothy Leonard, and Gary Hamel, "Change at Whirlpool Corporation (A)," *Harvard Business School Publishing*, 9-705-462, rev. March 6, 2006, p. 1, www.hbsp.harvard.edu (accessed December 3, 2010).

7 Edgar Schein, *Organizational Culture and Leadership*, The Jossey-Bass Business and Management Series (San Francisco: Jossey-Bass, 2010), pp. 307, 331.

Conclusion

1 www.napoleonguide.com (accessed August 28, 2012).

Index

About the Authors

Gregory P. Shea, PhD, consults, researches, writes, and teaches in the areas of organizational and individual change, group effectiveness, and conflict resolution. He is adjunct professor of management at the Wharton School of the University of Pennsylvania and of its Aresty Institute of Executive Education, adjunct senior fellow at the Leonard Davis Institute of Health Economics at Wharton, a faculty associate of the Wharton School's Center for Leadership and Change, president of Shea and Associates, Inc., senior consultant at CFAR, and a principal in the Coxe Group, an international consulting firm serving the design professions. He serves as the academic director for the Johnson & Johnson/Wharton CEO Program from Health Care Leadership and for the Johnson & Johnson/Wharton Fellows Program for Nurse Executives. His awards include an Excellence in Teaching Award from Wharton. He is a member of the Academy of Management and the American Psychological Association.

Shea's writing has appeared in such journals as the *Sloan Management Review, Journal of Applied Management, Journal of Applied Behavior Science, Journal of Conflict Resolution, British Journal of Social Psychology, Journal of Management Development*, and *Nursing Administration Quarterly*. He has also served as contributing editor to the *Journal of Applied Behavioral Science* and as a reviewer for *Group and Organization Management*,

Journal of Applied Psychology, Personnel Psychology, Personality and Social Psychology Bulletin, and *Psychology Bulletin.*

Shea is coauthor of *Your Job Survival Guide: A Manual for Thriving in Change.* He is a Phi Beta Kappa graduate of Harvard College and holds an MSc in management studies from the London School of Economics and an MA, MPhil, and PhD in administrative science from Yale University.

Cassie A. Solomon teaches leaders and organizations how to design and implement successful change. She is the president and founder of The New Group Consulting, Inc. Prior to starting her own company, she spent 16 years with CFAR. While there, she codirected the Hospitals and Health Care Systems practice. She is a principal in the Coxe Group international consultancy, a multidiscipline management consulting firm that serves the design profession, and she is on the faculty at WJM Associates. She is also an affiliate of Schaffer Consulting. Cassie is the author of a study of the successful adoption of new technology for the National Academies. She has taught health care executives at Wharton's Leonard Davis Institute and teaches change management to executives at Wharton's Aresty Institute. She is the creator of RACI Training, a method devoted to applying the RACI tool to help leaders work with and strengthen decision-making practices in their organizations. Cassie is an alumna of Yale University and the Wharton School of Business.

About Wharton Digital Press

Wharton Digital Press was established to inspire bold, insightful thinking within the global business community. In the tradition of The Wharton School of the University of Pennsylvania and its online business journal, *Knowledge@Wharton*, Wharton Digital Press uses innovative digital technologies to help managers meet the challenges of today and tomorrow.

As an entrepreneurial publisher, Wharton Digital Press delivers relevant, accessible, conceptually sound, and empirically based business knowledge to readers wherever and whenever they need it. Its format ranges from ebooks and enhanced ebooks to mobile apps and print books available through print-on-demand technology. Directed to a general business audience, the Press's areas of interest include management and strategy, innovation and entrepreneurship, finance and investment, leadership, marketing, operations, human resources, social responsibility, business-government relations, and more.

wdp.wharton.upenn.edu

Wharton
UNIVERSITY *of* PENNSYLVANIA

About The Wharton School

The Wharton School of the University of Pennsylvania—
founded in 1881 as the first collegiate business school—is
recognized globally for intellectual leadership and ongoing
innovation across every major discipline of business education.
The most comprehensive source of business knowledge in the
world, Wharton bridges research and practice through its broad
engagement with the global business community. The School
has more than 4,800 undergraduate, MBA, executive MBA,
and doctoral students; more than 9,000 annual participants in
executive education programs; and an alumni network of 86,000
graduates.

www.wharton.upenn.edu

CPSIA information can be obtained at www.ICGtesting.com
Printed in the USA
LVOW13s2309140514

385690LV00001B/2/P